BENJAMIN *Harrison*

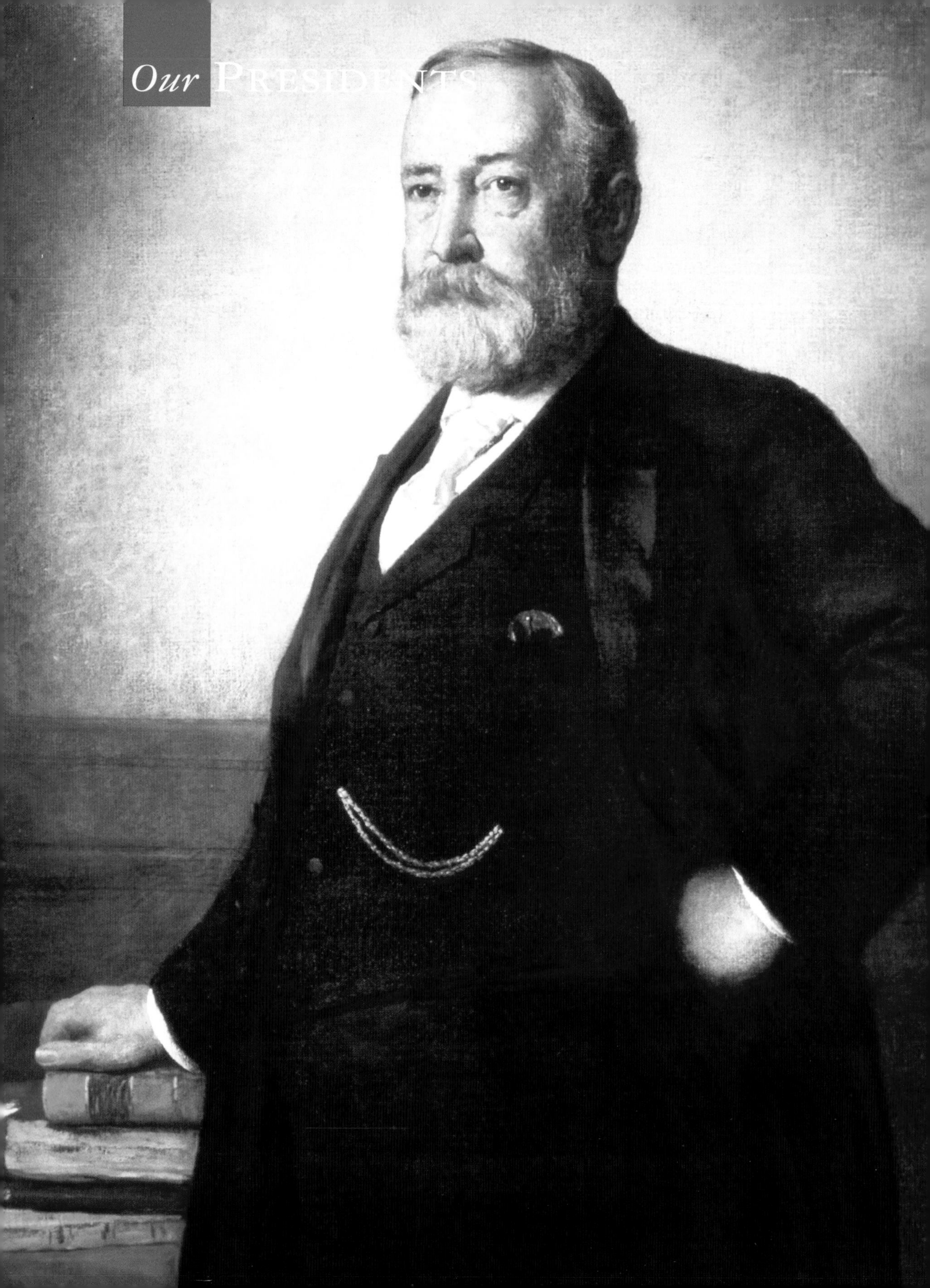

BENJAMIN *Harrison*

OUR TWENTY-THIRD PRESIDENT

By Sandra Francis

SPIRIT
of America®

The Child's World®
Chanhassen, Minnesota

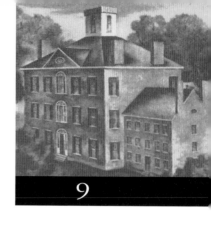

9

BENJAMIN *Harrison*

Published in the United States of America by The Child's World®
PO Box 326 • Chanhassen, MN 55317-0326 • 800-599-READ • www.childsworld.com

Acknowledgments
The Creative Spark: Mary Francis-DeMarois, Project Director; Elizabeth Sirimarco Budd, Series Editor; Robert Court, Design and Art Direction; Janine Graham, Page Layout; Jennifer Moyers, Production

The Child's World®: Mary Berendes, Publishing Director; Red Line Editorial, Fact Research; Cindy Klingel, Curriculum Advisor; Robert Noyed, Historical Advisor

Photos
Cover: White House Collection, courtesy White House Historical Association; Courtesy of the Benjamin Harrison Home, Indianapolis, Indiana: 6, 7, 10, 11, 13, 14, 17, 18, 22, 23, 26, 28, 29, 30, 31, 33, 34, 35, 36, 37; Courtesy of Berkeley Plantation, Charles City, Virginia: 8; Corbis: 27; Lake County Historical Society, Mentor, Ohio: 25 (house); Collections of the Library of Congress: 6, 15, 19, 21 (both images), 25 (inset); Courtesy of Miami University, Oxford Ohio: 9; Rutherford B. Hayes Presidential Center, Fremont, OH: 24

Registration
The Child's World®, Spirit of America®, and their associated logos are the sole property and registered trademarks of The Child's World®.

Library of Congress Cataloging-in-Publication Data
Francis, Sandra.
    Benjamin Harrison : our twenty-third president / by Sandra Francis.
        p. cm.
    Includes bibliographical references and index.
    ISBN 1-56766-860-7 (alk. paper)
    1. Harrison, Benjamin, 1833–1901—Juvenile literature. 2.Presidents—United States—
Biography—Juvenile literature. [1. Harrison, Benjamin, 1833–1901. 2. Presidents.] I. Title.
    E702 .F73 2001
    973.8'6'092—dc21
                                                        00-011458

Contents

Chapter ONE

A Family of Leaders

Benjamin Harrison was the nation's 23rd president. Few other presidents have had such a long family history of service to the U.S. government.

BENJAMIN HARRISON'S FAMILY WAS INVOLVED in the U.S. government long before he became the 23rd president. His grandfather had been among the men who signed the Declaration of Independence. William Henry Harrison, Benjamin's grandfather, was the nation's ninth president. The family tradition of entering politics—the work of the government— seemed to strike every generation. Benjamin's father, John Scott Harrison, served as a representative to Congress from the state of Ohio.

Benjamin was born on his grandfather's Ohio farm on August 20, 1833. He was the second of 10 children. Soon Benjamin's grandfather gave his father a piece of land to farm. It was a large, fertile strip located at the

place where the Ohio and the Big Miami rivers came together. The family called their farm The Point.

John Harrison built a large brick house at The Point. He also built a log schoolhouse for his growing family. With their own private teachers and their grandfather's vast history library, the Harrison children received a good education.

Religion and family activities were important to the Harrison family. Sundays were

Benjamin Harrison was born at his grandfather's farm in North Bend, Ohio. In 1789, his grandparents bought the land where it was built. At that time, Ohio was still considered the frontier, a wild region beyond settled lands.

7

spent at church services, which were often followed by family gatherings. Ben and his brothers worked hard on the farm. After growing and harvesting the crops, they hauled them to the river. There they loaded the crops on flatboats and shipped them to New Orleans. Ben was small for his age, but he often took the lead in the hardest work.

Whenever there was time, the Harrison children went fishing and swimming in the river. Ben was an excellent fisherman and hunter. He often provided food for his family. He also enjoyed playing rough games. He wanted to prove that he could be just as strong as his larger brothers.

At age 14, Ben enrolled at Farmers' College in Ohio. There he became friends with Caroline Scott, whom he called Carrie. She was the daughter of Dr. John Scott, a former teacher at the school. Ben later decided to finish his studies at Miami University in Oxford, Ohio. That same year, Carrie became a student at Oxford Female College. After a time, they realized that they wanted to spend the rest of their lives together. They

Harrison was named after his great-grandfather, Benjamin, who was a former governor of Virginia and was also among the patriots who signed the Declaration of Independence.

were still too young to marry, but they became engaged. Carrie continued her studies in art and music at Oxford. Ben finished his education in law and religion. He graduated from Miami University in 1852.

Harrison went to Miami University in Oxford, Ohio. The school was founded in 1809.

While home at The Point for a vacation, Ben learned that his father had borrowed money to pay for his schooling. Now he had to sell some of his land to pay back what he owed. Ben hadn't known how difficult it had been for his father to pay for his schooling. He decided to finish his education by working as an **apprentice** for a lawyer. This meant he would learn by experience while he worked. He studied in a Cincinnati law office, and by spring of 1854, Ben passed his law exams. He was then qualified to work as a lawyer.

Meanwhile, John Harrison had been elected a representative to the U.S. Congress.

9

He would have to move to Washington, D.C., to take the position. Although he wanted to go very much, John worried about leaving The Point. His wife had died a few years earlier. He still had young children at home with no mother to raise them.

Ben was proud of his father and wanted to find a solution. He and Carrie decided to wed and then live at The Point. They would care for the rest of the family. On October 20, 1853, Carrie and Ben married. That December, John Harrison accepted his duties in the House of Representatives.

Harrison's mother, Elizabeth, died while he was still in his teens. His father, John, took charge of raising their 12 children all by himself.

Ben loved living at The Point. But to be successful as a lawyer, he knew he would have to live in a busy city. Later, one of his brothers returned to the farm to live and took over the tasks of caring for the children and the farm. Now Ben and Carrie had to decide where to live. Family and friends encouraged them to settle in Cincinnati. The Harrison family was already well known there, which would help him open a law office. But Ben wanted to be recognized for his own accomplishments, not those of his famous family.

In 1854, he visited Indianapolis, the capital of Indiana. It was growing rapidly, yet still had the feel of a smaller country town. Ben's cousin, William Sheets, lived there. He was a well-known, successful businessman. Having little money, Ben and Carrie gratefully accepted an invitation to live in his cousin's home until they found their own. When Carrie learned that she was expecting their first child, she returned to Oxford to live with her parents until the baby was born. Their first

Harrison decided to move to Indianapolis to seek his fortune. It took a few years for him to make a name for himself, but he later ran the busy and successful law office shown above.

▸ Harrison's grandfather, William Henry, was the last president born before the start of the American Revolution.

▸ As a young boy, Harrison cut wood and carried water for the family so their cook would have time to fish and hunt with him.

▸ As an adult, Harrison was just five feet, seven inches tall. Only one other president was shorter: James Madison, the nation's fourth president.

child, Russell Benjamin Harrison, was born on August 12, 1854. Ben worked hard to earn more money. He wanted to bring his wife and child back to a place of their own.

It was difficult to attract clients, but Ben soon had a change of luck. He took a job with the court for $2.50 a day. The pay was small, but it allowed him to meet other lawyers. They began to pay him to help prepare their cases. Soon Ben was well known for his excellent courtroom speeches. By 1855, he was working with another attorney named William Wallace. Together, they built a successful law practice. With Ben's career established, Carrie and Russell returned to Indianapolis. Ben moved his family to a larger, more comfortable house. A second child, Mary (Mamie) Scott Harrison was born April 3, 1858. Unfortunately, Ben was often too busy to spend much time with his family.

At age 24, Ben accepted the position of city attorney. In this position, he took charge of legal matters for the city. Then he was elected reporter of the Indiana **Supreme Court** in 1860. It was not only an important position, but it paid well, too. The Harrisons were in Indianapolis to stay.

LITTLE BENJAMIN HARRISON spent many hours in the **campaign** headquarters of his grandfather, William Henry Harrison. The famous 1840 presidential campaign is said to have been one of the "noisiest, jolliest runs for the office of president in United States history." His grandfather was nicknamed "Old Tippecanoe" because of his victory against Native Americans in the Battle of Tippecanoe of 1811. A man named John Tyler was running for vice president. "Tippecanoe and Tyler, too" became one of the most famous campaign slogans in American history.

William Henry Harrison eventually won the campaign. His **inauguration** took place on March 4, 1841. It was a cold, rainy day. A huge crowd was there to witness the event. In fact, it was the biggest crowd since George Washington had taken the oath of office some 50 years earlier. Even in such bad weather, Harrison gave the longest inaugural speech in history—a full two hours! Later that day, he came down with a cold.

Unfortunately, William Henry Harrison had the misfortune to become the first president to die in office. His cold quickly grew more serious. Just one month after he became president, Harrison died of **pneumonia.** His was the shortest presidency in U.S. history.

Chapter TWO

A Call to War

Harrison's bravery in the Civil War made him a hero. Although he regretted leaving his family to fight for the Union, he fought fiercely and led his troops to many victories.

WHILE BENJAMIN HARRISON WAS BUSY building a successful law practice, the issue of slavery was tearing the nation apart. More and more people in the North were against it. But Southerners refused to give up their slaves. They were sure they could never run their large farms, called plantations, without the free labor the slaves provided. By the early 1860s, it appeared that the country could not avoid a **civil war.**

In April of 1861, the South fired on Fort Sumter, a U.S. fort in South Carolina. Harrison wanted to join the **Union** forces at once and fight for his country, just as his famous grandfather had. President Lincoln issued an urgent request for 6,000 volunteer soldiers from Indiana. When 12,000 men

14

signed on, Harrison decided that he should stay with his family and continue practicing law.

The conflict between the North and the South continued to rage, but the number of men who were joining the army decreased. By July of 1862, Harrison knew it was time for him to go to war. The governor of Indiana asked Harrison to **recruit** men into the army. Lieutenant Harrison's first recruit was his law partner and friend, William Wallace. By August 8, Harrison, now a colonel, had recruited 1,000 men. They became known as the 70th Indiana Regiment.

The Civil War began when the Confederates—soldiers from the South—attacked Fort Sumter in 1861.

Harrison and his troops traveled to Kentucky, where they trained as soldiers and prepared to face the enemy. Harrison had little military knowledge. With his own money, he hired an expert soldier to help him. He spent his days learning to give his troops the best possible training. In the evenings, he read books about military **strategy** and wrote letters to Carrie.

For nearly two years, the 70th Indiana Regiment guarded the Union railways in Kentucky and Tennessee. Harrison's hard work paid off in his first real battle. He and his men defeated a band of **Confederate** soldiers in Kentucky. A surprise attack trapped the enemy troops, and the 70th Regiment captured their supplies and horses. They returned to their post, pleased with their success.

For a time, Harrison and his men saw little action until the army ordered them to march south toward Atlanta, Georgia. It was not an easy march. The officers in charge had horses to ride, but the other soldiers had to walk. Many of the men became sick and weak. Colonel Harrison got down from his own horse more then once to let an ill soldier ride.

16

His kindness and concern made his soldiers respect and admire their leader.

At last, in January of 1864, Harrison and his men were called to join the troops of Generals William Sherman and Ulysses S. Grant. Their goal was to seize Atlanta. Colonel Harrison was not as experienced as other Union leaders, but he led his troops in two great victories. In the first battle, they charged over difficult ground to drive Confederate troops from the town of Resaca. This victory was the first step in capturing Atlanta.

Harrison led his troops in the Battle of Resaca in Georgia. This was an important step in the Union army's goal to capture Atlanta.

Harrison was called to fight in many more battles. The Confederates decided to attack Sherman's forces in late July of 1864. They hoped to divide the Union troops in half and make them less powerful. Harrison quickly mounted his horse, shouting, "Come on, boys, we're not licked yet!" He then led his men to victory. After this battle, called the Battle of Peachtree Creek, Harrison was made a brigadier general. He also became known as a hero. By September 1, the Union troops had driven the Confederates out of Atlanta.

Because his grandfather was known as an excellent soldier, people expected a great deal from Benjamin Harrison during the Civil War. As it turned out, he fought more battles in six months than his grandfather did in his entire life. Harrison became known for his bravery and was promoted to the rank of brigadier general. He is shown here at far left with Union Generals Ward, Dustin, and Cogswell.

Afterward, General Sherman gave them a well-deserved rest. Indiana's governor requested that Harrison be sent to Indianapolis for special duty. The assignment gave him a short reunion with his family.

While he was away, another man had taken over Harrison's position as reporter of the Supreme Court. The governor wanted Harrison to campaign to win back the position. He also asked him to recruit more Indiana men for the Union army. News of Harrison's heroism in Georgia had spread throughout Indiana, so it was easy for him to recruit men. He also campaigned for President Abraham Lincoln, who was running for a second **term** as president. Both Harrison and Lincoln won in the November elections.

In December of 1864, Harrison and his men returned to duty. Their job was to drive Confederate General John Hood out of Tennessee. Their victory ended the war in that state. For his efforts, Harrison received

In the capture of Atlanta, Harrison led his troops to two great victories. The most famous was the Battle of Peachtree Creek. When Confederates tried to drive between the Union troops to separate them, Harrison quickly charged his men into battle, shouting, "Come on boys, we're not licked yet!" Running the Confederates out of the area was a major victory for the Union.

19

a second leave of duty, which allowed him to return home for a brief time.

After a short visit, Harrison went to South Carolina, where he trained replacement troops for a few months. In April, he planned to rejoin his regiment in North Carolina. On the way, he learned that Confederate General Robert E. Lee's army had **surrendered.** Soon the war would be over and the Union saved. Huge celebrations took place for days. But then tragedy struck the nation. Just six days later, on April 14, 1865, President Lincoln was **assassinated.**

Harrison arrived in North Carolina on the same day that news of the tragedy reached the people. The streets were empty, for the South had been devastated by the war. In the Union camps, flags hung sadly at half-mast in honor of President Lincoln. When Harrison learned that Lincoln was dead, he was shocked and full of grief. By request, he delivered a speech at a memorial service honoring the president.

On May 24, 1865, a parade took place in Washington, D.C., to celebrate the end of the war and to honor the troops who saved the

Union. Harrison and the 70th Indiana Regiment fell in line and proudly marched as heroes behind General Sherman. But before they did, Harrison gave a speech to his men. With great sincerity, he said, "The highest honors are due to the men who bore the cartridge and the gun. What were your officers without you?"

The happy events celebrating the Union's victory came to an abrupt end when President Lincoln was assassinated. Hundreds of people marched in his funeral procession. People lined the streets to show their respect for the great leader.

Chapter THREE

A Worthy Candidate

At the end of the Civil War, Harrison was happy to return to Indianapolis. He hoped to spend as much time as possible with his family. But soon his career would again occupy most of his days.

ON JUNE 8, 1865, HARRISON LEFT THE ARMY. He was happy to return to his life as a husband, father, and lawyer. The years he had spent away from home took a toll on his marriage and family life. He felt that he hardly knew his children. Russell was now 10 years old, and Mamie was seven. Harrison wanted to spend less time working and more time with his family. Together they enjoyed taking rides in their horse-drawn buggy and socializing with friends at church dinners. He took his son on fishing trips. He and Mrs. Harrison went to the theater and the opera.

It was not long before Harrison was back in the habit of working too hard, however. He gained weight and often complained of not feeling well.

In April of 1867, he became so exhausted that he couldn't work for several weeks. Something had to change, so he decided to give up the tiring position of reporter. After a relaxing fishing trip in Minnesota, Harrison was ready to return to his law practice. But he also hoped one day to continue his career in politics.

After the war, Harrison made an effort to devote more time to his wife, Carrie, but his career was still very important to him. He hoped to enter politics.

In 1872, Harrison believed he was ready to run for governor of Indiana. He was a member of the Republican Party, one of the two major U.S. **political parties.** He hoped the Republicans would choose him as their **candidate** for governor, but they did not. In 1876, he again hoped to run for governor. This time, he won the Republican **nomination** but lost the election. Still, the campaign brought him to the attention of Indiana's citizens.

Except for the death of Harrison's father, the 1870s were good years for the family. In 1875, they built a lovely home in Indianapolis. Mrs. Harrison planted gardens and enjoyed taking care of them. Mamie grew into a pretty and popular young woman. Russell graduated from Lafayette College.

In 1879, President Rutherford B. Hayes (below) appointed Harrison to the Mississippi River Commission. This group was charged with deciding how the river could be used. The commission never accomplished anything, so it was done away with in 1881. Although the project was a loss, Harrison met many important people, bringing him one step closer to a career in national politics.

In 1880, Indiana Republicans sent Harrison to the Republican National Convention in Chicago. The purpose of this large meeting was to select the Republican candidate for the next presidential election. Several men were being considered, but no one was the favorite. The men at the convention voted 33 times before they came to a decision. At last, they selected James A. Garfield of Ohio. Throughout Garfield's campaign, Harrison traveled around Indiana and other states, giving speeches that helped the Republicans win the presidency. Benjamin Harrison became known and respected throughout the nation.

In 1881, Harrison was elected to the U.S. Senate. President Garfield offered him a position in his **cabinet,** but Harrison refused it. He believed that his abilities would be more valuable in the Senate. He also thought it was a better place to reach his own goals in politics. For one thing, Harrison felt he could meet other important leaders who might offer him their support in future elections.

The Harrisons moved to Washington, where they would live for the next six years. But in their first year there, tragedy struck the nation again. President Garfield was assassinated, and Vice President Chester A. Arthur became president. Harrison did not have a good relationship with Arthur. When it was time to select a candidate for the next presidential election, Harrison campaigned for James G. Blaine of Maine. Blaine was chosen as the Republican candidate, but he did not win the presidency. Grover Cleveland, who belonged to the Democratic Party, won the election.

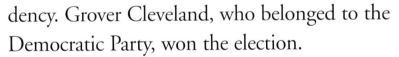

Six years in the Senate taught Harrison how the United States political system worked. His career was enjoyable, except for the daily stream of people who came to him asking for jobs or favors. Harrison did not believe in giving jobs to people who were not qualified to do the work. He always agreed to meet with **veterans** of the army, however. He supported these men until the end of his life. Harrison was known as someone who would help those who had once fought for their country.

In 1880, Harrison helped James Garfield (shown above) campaign for the presidency. Garfield's home was the site of a successful "front-porch campaign," which is one that takes place at a candidate's home. People traveled to Garfield's home in Ohio to hear him give speeches. His supporters, including Benjamin Harrison, traveled around the country, encouraging Americans to vote for Garfield.

Harrison spent six years in the Senate. During this time, many people in the Republican Party began to think he would make an excellent candidate for the presidency.

As a member of the Committee on Military Affairs, he supported efforts aimed at building a stronger, more modern navy.

Senator Harrison also helped pass a **bill** that created a new government in the **territory** of Alaska. Before that time, the military had controlled it. Now the people who lived there could take control of their government. Harrison wanted many of the territories in the West to become states. He helped lay the groundwork for this to take place in future years. He also tried to protect a beautiful site on the Colorado River known as the Grand Canyon. Harrison was the first senator to suggest making this area a national park.

Harrison accomplished much during his six years in the Senate. But while he was away, members of the Democratic Party replaced the Republicans in Indiana's state government. In 1887, Harrison was not reelected to the Senate. He was sorry to lose his position, but he was now free to pursue his greatest career goal—the presidency. In 1888, he became a candidate for that office.

SENATOR HARRISON ADMIRED ARIZONA'S GRAND CANYON AND BELIEVED THE U.S. government should protect this natural wonder. He wanted Congress to create a national park in the region. The national parks are public grounds set aside for people to visit and enjoy. They preserve wilderness and honor important events in history. Yellowstone, located in Wyoming and Montana, was the first national park, created in 1872.

Senator Harrison introduced bills in 1882, 1883, and again in 1886 to establish the Grand Canyon National Park. His fellow lawmakers refused to pass them. Although Harrison was not able to reach this goal while he was in the Senate, his efforts eventually paid off. As president, Harrison created the Grand Canyon Forest Reserve, a first step toward his goal. Finally, in 1918, Congress passed a bill establishing the Grand Canyon National Park. President Woodrow Wilson signed it into law on February 26, 1919.

Chapter FOUR

The Centennial President

Like Garfield before him, Harrison stayed home and let the people come to him during his campaign. Nearly 300,000 people visited the Harrisons' home in Indiana to hear him give speeches from his front porch.

AFTER A COLORFUL CAMPAIGN, BENJAMIN Harrison was elected president of the United States. His 1889 inauguration took place 100 years after George Washington entered office, so Harrison became known as the "Centennial President." A centennial is a 100th anniversary.

Harrison won the election, but it was a very close vote. He received 100,000 fewer votes from the American people than President Grover Cleveland did. But he won 233 **electoral votes,** while Cleveland won only 168. Although many Americans wanted Cleveland to stay in office, Harrison became the new leader. The people of Indiana were proud of him. As he prepared to leave for Washington, they gave him a grand send-off.

On a cold and rainy day in the nation's capital, Benjamin Harrison became the 23rd president of the United States. His first job was to choose a cabinet. President Harrison selected men with experience. Whenever he had to make important decisions such as this, he refused to let others tell him what to do. This angered many important Republicans. They wanted him to take their advice. As a result, Harrison lost their support.

Harrison's inauguration took place on March 4, 1889, a rainy and cold day. Even in such bad weather, a huge crowd gathered for the event. Grover Cleveland, the outgoing president, held an umbrella over Harrison's head as he took the oath of office.

Harrison (center) posed for this portrait with his cabinet. When he became president, many people asked him for positions in the government. Harrison said that filling the positions was a "frightful ordeal." Most people who asked for jobs were "worthy men and many of them are personal friends." But he could not aid every person who sought his help.

Harrison had many goals he hoped to achieve. He was one of the first presidents to succeed in foreign affairs, which are matters involving other countries. His work brought about better relations with other nations. He wanted to build friendships with other countries on the American continents. To achieve this, the first Pan-American Congress met in Washington, D.C., in 1889. Representatives from many countries attended the meeting.

President Harrison led the way for six territories to enter the Union. The Omnibus Bill of 1889 allowed North Dakota, South Dakota, Montana, and Washington to become states. Wyoming and Idaho became states in 1890. Harrison also asked the Senate to make Hawaii a U.S. territory. Unfortunately, the next president stopped this from happening when he took office. Harrison was greatly disappointed by this.

Harrison and many congressmen also wanted to pass the Force Bill. It would have provided government protection to black

The White House was in a terrible state when Harrison became president. In fact, there was talk of replacing it with a new mansion for the president. Finally, the government decided to repair the historic home.

▸ When there was talk of building a new president's mansion, Mrs. Harrison threw herself into the project with enthusiasm. Then the government decided to repair the White House instead. She led the efforts to refurbish it, using $35,000 that the government had set aside for the project.

▸ President and Mrs. Harrison were the first residents of the White House to have electricity. But they didn't like the electric lights that were installed. In fact, the president refused to touch the switch, afraid that he might be shocked.

voters during elections in the South. After the Civil War, white people often threatened blacks who tried to vote. They even created state laws to stop them from voting. The House of Representatives passed the Force Bill. Unfortunately, the Senate refused to pass it, so it did not become a law.

One victory during Harrison's term was the Dependent Pension Act, passed in 1890. It granted money to veterans who had been permanently injured in battle. Harrison and his advisors also continued a huge shipbuilding program. This helped build superior naval forces for the United States.

One of the most important achievements during Harrison's time in office was the Sherman Anti-Trust Act of 1890. This law allowed the government to make sure companies ran their businesses fairly. It stopped the most powerful companies in the nation from creating **trusts,** which are partnerships between large companies that are formed to put smaller ones out of business. Harrison and members of Congress wanted to help all American businesses succeed. Another way to accomplish this was the McKinley Tariff.

Harrison's grandson, also named Benjamin, lived at the White House with his family during the early 1890s. Little Benjamin was often photographed as he drove his goat cart about the grounds. The goat once ran away with the boy and raced down the White House driveway, onto Pennsylvania Avenue. The president himself, dressed in a top hat and long black coat, ran after them in hot pursuit.

A tariff is a tax on foreign goods to make them cost more. Congress hoped the McKinley Tariff would make Americans buy more products made in the United States. Unfortunately, many people did not like the tariff and the higher prices it created. It made Harrison and many Republicans in Congress unpopular with the people and hurt their chances for reelection.

Even though he had lost a lot of support from the Republican Party, Harrison was nominated to run for a second term. Mrs. Harrison became very ill during this time.

In the summer of 1891, Mrs. Harrison developed a bad cough. She became much weaker the following year. Soon she could not leave her bed. Doctors said she had tuberculosis, a serious disease that affects the lungs. Unfortunately, she never recovered.

When the president learned that she did not have long to live, he refused to leave her side to campaign for office. On October 25, 1892, his beloved Carrie died at the White House.

Most Americans wanted to elect a Democrat as the next president. Grover Cleveland won the election. He became the only president ever to be reelected after being voted out of office.

When Harrison received the news that he had lost the election, he was too sad about Mrs. Harrison's death to care. "Political defeat carries no personal grief," he said. After Cleveland's inauguration, Harrison returned to Indianapolis. He continued to work as a lawyer and spent many hours writing articles for magazines and newspapers. He also wrote a book titled *This Country of Ours*.

After being alone for three years, Harrison married a young widow, Mary Lord Dimmick, who was Carrie's niece. Soon they had a child, whom they named Elizabeth. The marriage and new baby gave Harrison great joy. His Republican friends hinted that he should run for president again. Harrison was not interested. He said a new "pilot could steer the Ship of State more satisfactorily."

Harrison continued working until his death from pneumonia on March 13, 1901. His wife and many friends were at his bedside. His body was placed in the Indiana State House, where the survivors of the 70th

Harrison married Mary Lord Dimmick in late 1895. She is shown here with their daughter, Elizabeth.

▶ Benjamin Harrison
was happy to finally
leave politics and lead
a quiet life. He once
said, "For nearly 60
years of my life, I was
driven by work. I want
hereafter to do the
driving myself."

Indiana Regiment led soldiers and citizens in a parade to honor him.

Many people expressed their admiration for Harrison. They also expressed their sorrow for his death. Perhaps ex-president Grover Cleveland best described the excellence of Harrison's life when he said, "In public office he was guided by patriotism and devotion to duty—often at the sacrifice of temporary popularity—and in private [life] his influence and example were always in the direction of decency and good citizenship."

*Benjamin Harrison is
remembered as an honest
president who always
tried to do what he
believed was right.*

Copyright 1889

FOUR GENERATIONS lived in the White House during President Harrison's term. The oldest was 90-year-old Dr. John Scott, Carrie Harrison's father. Mamie came with her two children, Benjamin Harrison McKee and Mary Lodge McKee. Mamie helped her mother with the huge task of entertaining visitors to the White House. Mamie's husband, Bob, traveled between his business in Indianapolis and his family in the White House. The president's son, Russell, traveled between Washington, D.C., and his ranch and newspaper business in Montana. His wife, Mary, and daughter, Marthena, lived with the rest of the Harrisons at the White House. Mary helped Carrie Harrison manage the household staff. Mrs. Harrison's widowed niece, Mary Lord Dimmick, also lived there. She helped with the chore of writing letters. In this photograph, Mrs. Harrison is holding little Benjamin McKee, Mamie stands in the center, and Dr. Scott is holding Mary McKee.

1833 Benjamin Harrison is born on August 20 on the farm of his grandfather, William Henry Harrison. Benjamin is the second of 10 children born to John and Elizabeth Harrison.

1847 At age 14, Harrison enters Farmers' College near Cincinnati.

1851 Harrison transfers to Miami University in Oxford, Ohio, to finish his education.

1852 Harrison graduates from Miami University.

1853 Harrison's father, John, is elected to Congress and must move to Washington, D.C. Benjamin Harrison and Caroline Scott marry and move to The Point (Harrison's childhood home). They care for Harrison's younger brothers and sisters who still live at home. Harrison travels to Cincinnati each day to study law.

1854 Harrison passes his law exams and visits Indianapolis. He decides to start his law career there. He and his wife move to Indianapolis. Their son, Russell, is born.

1855 Harrison forms a law partnership with William Wallace.

1857 Harrison becomes the city attorney of Indianapolis.

1858 The Harrisons' daughter, Mary (Mamie) Scott, is born.

1860 Harrison is elected reporter of the Indiana Supreme Court.

1861 The Civil War begins when the South fires on Fort Sumter.

1862 Harrison joins the army and becomes a lieutenant. He recruits men for the 70th Indiana Regiment, and his troops are sent to Kentucky and Tennessee to protect railroads for the next two years.

1864 Colonel Harrison and his men join Generals Sherman and Grant to capture Atlanta. Harrison leads his men to important victories at the Battles of Resaca and Peachtree Creek. He earns a promotion to brigadier general. In November, Harrison is reelected as reporter of the Indiana Supreme Court.

1865 The Confederates surrender, and the Civil War ends. On April 14, President Lincoln is assassinated.

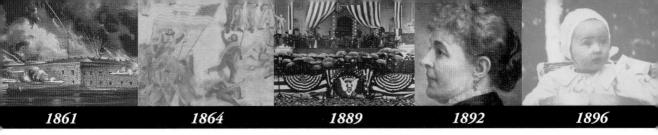

1875 Harrison and Carrie build a home in Indianapolis. It remains the family home until Harrison's death.

1876 Harrison wins the nomination for governor of Indiana, but he loses the election.

1880 Harrison attends the Republican National Convention in Chicago to select a presidential candidate.

1881 Harrison is elected to the U.S. Senate. President Garfield offers him a position in his cabinet, but Harrison refuses it. Later in the year, Garfield is assassinated.

1882 Senator Benjamin Harrison introduces the first bill to create Grand Canyon National Park. Congress does not pass it.

1887 Harrison is not reelected to the U.S. Senate.

1888 Harrison is elected the 23rd president of the United States.

1889 Harrison is inaugurated on March 4. The first Pan-American Congress meets in Washington. The Omnibus Bill allows North Dakota, South Dakota, Montana, and Washington to become states.

1890 The House passes the Force Bill to protect African American voters in the South; however, the Senate refuses to pass it. The Dependent Pension Act is passed to give money to veterans injured in war. The Sherman Anti-Trust Act prevents big businesses from creating trusts. The McKinley Tariff is enacted to make Americans buy more products made in the United States. Wyoming and Idaho are admitted to the Union.

1892 The Republican Party nominates Harrison to run for a second term. Carrie Harrison dies shortly before the presidential election. Harrison loses the election to Grover Cleveland.

1893 President Harrison creates the Grand Canyon Forest Reserve before leaving office.

1895 Harrison marries Mary Lord Dimmick.

1896 The Harrisons' daughter, Elizabeth, is born.

1901 Benjamin Harrison dies on March 13. The survivors of the 70th Indiana Regiment lead soldiers in a parade to honor their leader.

apprentice (uh-PREN-tiss)
An apprentice promises to work for a skilled worker in exchange for learning a business. Harrison decided to study law as an apprentice to a lawyer.

assassinate (uh-SASS-uh-nayt)
Assassinate means to murder someone, especially a well-known person. President Abraham Lincoln was assassinated on April 14, 1865.

bill (BILL)
A bill is an idea for a new law that is presented to a group of lawmakers. Harrison helped pass a bill that created a new government in Alaska.

cabinet (KAB-eh-net)
A cabinet is the group of people who advise a president. President Garfield offered Harrison a post in his cabinet.

campaign (kam-PAYN)
A campaign is the process of running for an election, including activities such as giving speeches or attending rallies. Harrison was fascinated by his grandfather's campaign for the presidency.

candidate (KAN-dih-det)
A candidate is a person running for office. In 1872, Harrison hoped to be the Republican candidate for governor of Indiana.

civil war (SIV-il WAR)
A civil war is a war between opposing groups of citizens within the same country. The American Civil War began in 1861.

Confederate (kun-FED-ur-ut)
Confederate refers to the slave states (or the people who lived in those states) that left the Union in 1861. The people of the South were called Confederates.

electoral votes (ee-LEKT-uh-rul VOHTZ)
Electoral votes are votes cast by representatives of the American public. Each state chooses representatives who vote for a candidate in a presidential election. These representatives are supposed to vote according to what most people in their state want.

inauguration (ih-nawg-yuh-RAY-shun)
An inauguration is the ceremony that takes place when a new president begins a term. Harrison's inauguration took place on March 4, 1889.

nomination (nom-ih-NAY-shun)
If someone receives a nomination, he or she is chosen by a political party to run for an office. Harrison won the Republican presidential nomination in 1888.

Glossary TERMS

pneumonia (noo-MOH-nyuh)
Pneumonia is a disease that causes swelling of the lungs, high fever, and difficulty breathing. Harrison died of pneumonia.

**political parties
(puh-LIT-uh-kul PAR-teez)**
Political parties are groups of people who share similar ideas about how to run a government. Harrison belonged to the Republican political party.

recruit (ree-KREWT)
If people recruit others to a group, they encourage them to join it. The governor of Indiana asked Harrison to recruit men into the army.

strategy (STRAT-eh-gee)
Strategy is skillful planning to achieve a goal. Harrison read books about military strategy to become a better leader.

**supreme court
(suh-PREEM KORT)**
A supreme court is the most powerful court in an individual state. Harrison was elected reporter for the Indiana Supreme Court.

surrender (suh-REN-dur)
If an army surrenders, it gives up to its enemy. The Confederates surrendered in 1865, ending the Civil War.

term (TERM)
A term is the length of time a politician can keep his or her position by law. A U.S. president's term of office is four years.

territory (TAYR-ih-tor-ee)
A territory is a land or region, especially land that belongs to a government. Harrison encouraged the government to grant statehood to territories.

trusts (TRUSTS)
Trusts are two or more companies that agree to work together. Trusts try to put other companies out of business to get more business for themselves.

union (YOON-yen)
A union is the joining together of two people or groups of people, such as states. The Union is another name for the United States.

veterans (VET-ur-enz)
Veterans are people who have served in the armed forces. Harrison worked to help veterans.

Our PRESIDENTS

President	Birthplace	Life Dates	Term	Political Party	First Lady
George Washington	Virginia	1732–1799	1789–1797	None	Martha Dandridge Custis Washington
John Adams	Massachusetts	1735–1826	1797–1801	Federalist	Abigail Smith Adams
Thomas Jefferson	Virginia	1743–1826	1801–1809	Democratic-Republican	widower
James Madison	Virginia	1751–1836	1809–1817	Democratic-Republican	Dolley Payne Todd Madison
James Monroe	Virginia	1758–1831	1817–1825	Democratic-Republican	Elizabeth "Eliza" Kortright Monroe
John Quincy Adams	Massachusetts	1767–1848	1825–1829	Democratic-Republican	Louisa Catherine Johnson Adams
Andrew Jackson	South Carolina	1767–1845	1829–1837	Democrat	widower
Martin Van Buren	New York	1782–1862	1837–1841	Democrat	widower
William Henry Harrison	Virginia	1773–1841	1841	Whig	Anna Tuthill Symmes Harrison
John Tyler	Virginia	1790–1862	1841–1845	Whig	Letitia Christian Tyler Julia Gardiner Tyler
James Polk	North Carolina	1795–1849	1845–1849	Democrat	Sarah Childress Polk

Our PRESENTS

President	Birthplace	Life Dates	Term	Political Party	First Lady
Zachary Taylor	Virginia	1784–1850	1849–1850	Whig	Margaret Mackall Smith Taylor
Millard Fillmore	New York	1800–1874	1850–1853	Whig	Abigail Powers Fillmore
Franklin Pierce	New Hampshire	1804–1869	1853–1857	Democrat	Jane Means Appleton Pierce
James Buchanan	Pennsylvania	1791–1868	1857–1861	Democrat	never married
Abraham Lincoln	Kentucky	1809–1865	1861–1865	Republican	Mary Todd Lincoln
Andrew Johnson	North Carolina	1808–1875	1865–1869	Democrat	Eliza McCardle Johnson
Ulysses S. Grant	Ohio	1822–1885	1869–1877	Republican	Julia Dent Grant
Rutherford B. Hayes	Ohio	1822–1893	1877–1881	Republican	Lucy Ware Webb Hayes
James A. Garfield	Ohio	1831–1881	1881	Republican	Lucretia Rudolph Garfield
Chester A. Arthur	Vermont	1829–1886	1881–1885	Republican	widower
Grover Cleveland	New Jersey	1837–1908	1885–1889	Democrat	Frances Folsom Cleveland

Our PRESENTS

Our PRESIDENTS

President	Birthplace	Life Dates	Term	Political Party	First Lady
Benjamin Harrison	Ohio	1833–1901	1889–1893	Republican	Caroline Lavina Scott Harrison
Grover Cleveland	New Jersey	1837–1908	1893–1897	Democrat	Frances Folsom Cleveland
William McKinley	Ohio	1843–1901	1897–1901	Republican	Ida Saxton McKinley
Theodore Roosevelt	New York	1858–1919	1901–1909	Republican	Edith Kermit Carow Roosevelt
William Howard Taft	Ohio	1857–1930	1909–1913	Republican	Helen Herron Taft
Woodrow Wilson	Virginia	1856–1924	1913–1921	Democrat	Ellen L. Axson Wilson Edith Bolling Galt Wilson
Warren G. Harding	Ohio	1865–1923	1921–1923	Republican	Florence Kling De Wolfe Harding
Calvin Coolidge	Vermont	1872–1933	1923–1929	Republican	Grace Anna Goodhue Coolidge
Herbert Hoover	Iowa	1874–1964	1929–1933	Republican	Lou Henry Hoover
Franklin D. Roosevelt	New York	1882–1945	1933–1945	Democrat	Anna Eleanor Roosevelt Roosevelt
Harry S. Truman	Missouri	1884–1972	1945–1953	Democrat	Elizabeth "Bess" Virginia Wallace Truman

Our PRESIDENTS

President	Birthplace	Life Dates	Term	Political Party	First Lady
Dwight D. Eisenhower	Texas	1890–1969	1953–1961	Republican	Mamie Geneva Doud Eisenhower
John F. Kennedy	Massachusetts	1917–1963	1961–1963	Democrat	Jacqueline Lee Bouvier Kennedy
Lyndon Baines Johnson	Texas	1908–1973	1963–1969	Democrat	Claudia "Lady Bird" Alta Taylor Johnson
Richard M. Nixon	California	1913–1994	1969–1974	Republican	Thelma "Pat" Catherine Patricia Ryan Nixon
Gerald R. Ford	Nebraska	1913–	1974–1977	Republican	Elizabeth "Betty" Bloomer Warren Ford
James Earl Carter	Georgia	1924–	1977–1981	Democrat	Rosalynn Smith Carter
Ronald Reagan	Illinois	1911–2004	1981–1989	Republican	Nancy Davis Reagan
George Bush	Massachusetts	1924–	1989–1993	Republican	Barbara Pierce Bush
William J. Clinton	Arkansas	1946–	1993–2001	Democrat	Hillary Rodham Clinton
George W. Bush	Connecticut	1946–	2001–	Republican	Laura Welch Bush

Presidential FACTS

Qualifications

To run for president, a candidate must
- be at least 35 years old
- be a citizen who was born in the United States
- have lived in the United States for 14 years

Term of Office

A president's term of office is four years. No president can stay in office for more than two terms.

Election Date

The presidential election takes place every four years on the first Tuesday of November.

Inauguration Date

Presidents are inaugurated on January 20.

Oath of Office

I do solemnly swear I will faithfully execute the office of the President of the United States and will to the best of my ability preserve, protect, and defend the Constitution of the United States.

Write a Letter to the President

One of the best things about being a U.S. citizen is that Americans get to participate in their government. They can speak out if they feel government leaders aren't doing their jobs. They can also praise leaders who are going the extra mile. Do you have something you'd like the president to do? Should the president worry more about the environment and encourage people to recycle? Should the government spend more money on our schools? You can write a letter to the president to say how you feel!

1600 Pennsylvania Avenue
Washington, D.C. 20500

You can even send an e-mail to: president@whitehouse.gov

For Further INFORMATION

Internet Sites

Visit the Benjamin Harrison Home:
http://www.surf-ici.com/harrison/

Read more about Harrison:
http://www.indianahistory.org/geib.htm
http://library.advanced.org/tq-admin/day.cgi

Examine a political cartoon about President Harrison:
http://www.surf-ici.com/harrison/cartoon.html

Read Harrison's inaugural address:
http://www.bartleby.com/124/pres38.html

Find historical resources about the Civil War, including time lines, historic figures, and life stories:
http://www.americancivilwar.com

Find a children's listing of other Civil War sites:
http://www.kidinfo.com/American_History/Civil_War.html

Learn more about the Grand Canyon:
http://www.grandcanyon.org/
http://www.kaibab.org/

Learn more about all the presidents and visit the White House:
http://www.whitehouse.gov/WH/glimpse/presidents/html/presidents.html
http://www.thepresidency.org/presinfo.htm
http://www.americanpresidents.org/

Books

Clinton, Susan. *Benjamin Harrison.* Chicago: Childrens Press, 1989.

Gaines, Ann Graham. *William Henry Harrison: Our Ninth President.* Chanhassen, MN: The Child's World, 2002.

Graham, Martin F., Richard A. Sauers, and George Skoch. *The Blue and the Gray.* Lincolnwood, IL: Publications International, 1996.

Rubel, David. *Scholastic Encyclopedia of the Presidents and Their Times.* New York: Scholastic, 1994.

Index